U0787757

春雨惊春清谷天
夏满芒夏暑相连
秋处露秋寒霜降
冬雪雪冬小大寒

本教材为 2016 年度教育部哲学社会科学研究重大课题攻关项目
“中国书法文化国际传播的理论与实践研究”（16JZD031）阶段性成果

二十四节气

春

風調雨順

Spring: Season with Timely Breeze and Rain for Crop Raising

The Twenty-four Solar Terms

主编：周斌 周佳楠
Editor-in-chief: ZHOU Bin, ZHOU Jianan

副主编：Roy Ye 尹冬民
Associate Editor: Roy Ye, YIN Dongmin

插图：孙凌雁
Illustrator:SUN Lingyan

书法：盛兰军
Calligraphy: SHENG Lanjun

翻译：胡子曦 Owen Pile
Translators: HU Zixi, Owen Pile

封面题字：Roy Ye
Calligraphy on the cover: Roy Ye

华东师范大学出版社

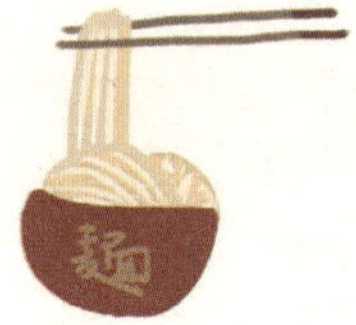

Nini is a China-bred panda. Jerry is one of her good friends who live in the United States. They write to each other every year. One year, Nini mailed an exquisite postcard to Jerry, which not only showed the Twenty-Four Solar Terms in the traditional Chinese lunar calendar, but also detailed the corresponding astrological signs. Jerry is tremendously fond of this card and asked Nini to tell him more about the Twenty-Four Solar Terms. This is how the story started.

熊猫妮妮从小生活在中国，她有一个好朋友叫杰瑞，住在美国。他们每年都写信问候彼此。有一年妮妮寄给杰瑞一张精美的卡片，卡片上不仅印着二十四节气，而且还有对照的星座图。杰瑞非常喜欢这张卡片，并请妮妮给他讲讲二十四节气的典故。故事就这样开始了……

二十四节气与十二星座对照图

The table of the Twenty-four Solar Terms and the corresponding astrological signs

Excuse me, Nini, what are the Twenty-four Solar Terms?

Hi, Jerry. There are four seasons in a year and each season includes six solar terms. Then there are Twenty-four Solar Terms in total throughout the whole year. Farmers in China design their schedule of farming according to the climate of every solar term. An old Chinese saying has it that "Plant your crops in spring, nurture them throughout summer, harvest them in autumn and rest your land in winter". This saying tells us the most fundamental rules of farming.

妮妮，什么是二十四节气呢？

杰瑞，一年有春、夏、秋、冬四个季节，每个季节都包含了六个节气，这样，一年中就有二十四个节气。有了这二十四节气，农民伯伯就可以根据每个节气的气候变化，安排自己的耕种时间。中国有一句古话叫作“春种夏长，秋收冬藏”，就体现了农业耕种的基本规律。

Contents

The Symphony of Spring

目 录

春季乐章

立春

Beginning of Spring
Li Chun

Important facts about Beginning of Spring

The story of **Beginning of Spring**

Beginning of Spring, which is also called "Da Chun", comes the first of the Twenty-Four Solar Terms. It comes between 3rd and 5th February every year. Beginning of Spring, as its name shows, is considered to be the start of the spring season. The period of time from Beginning of Spring to Beginning of Summer is the season of spring. After Beginning of Spring, the temperature starts to rise, and the land and the lakes start to thaw.

Changes happening after Beginning of Spring:

Ice melts away. Everything comes to life.
Winter jasmine blooms and all sorts of flowers are ready to come into blossom.
Fishes come to the surface of the water to welcome the advent of spring.

The customs on the day of Beginning of Spring: field trip to the outdoors, having a bite of the spring.

Tips

On this day, people eat spring rolls and spring pancakes as a form of celebration. This activity is called "Yao Chun" in Chinese, which means having a bite of spring.

立春的故事

立春大事记

立春是二十四节气之首，又称“打春”，时间点是在每年的2月3～5日之间。中国传统上把立春作为春季的开始，从这一天直到立夏，都被称为春天。立春之后气温开始回暖，土地、湖面也逐渐化冻。

立春变化

冰雪融化，万物复苏。
迎春花开，百花待放。
鱼儿出水，迎接春天。

立春风俗：春游、咬春

小贴士 在立春这一天，人们吃春饼和春卷庆祝节日，称为“咬春”。

the Spring Festival

On the Chinese lunar calendar, 1st January is the traditional Chinese Spring Festival, which is the most important festival to the people. The day right before the Spring Festival, which is also the last day of the year on the Chinese lunar calendar, is called "Chu Xi". "Chu Xi" is the day when everybody in a family comes back home for a reunion. Every family is busy decorating their house with the Spring Festival scrolls and red lanterns. People cook a New Year's Eve dinner, where dumplings are indispensable. Firecrackers and fireworks are favored particularly by children. In the days following the Spring Festival, families visit their friends and relatives, exchanging gifts. The younger generation needs to visit the elder generation and wish them good health, while the older generation gives the younger generation "lucky money" packed in red envelopes.

pasting Spring Festival scrolls

visiting relatives and friends

exchanging gifts

春节

农历的正月初一是“春节”，它是中国民间最重要的传统节日。春节的前一天，即农历一年的最后一天，被称为“除夕”，这一天是全家团圆的日子，家家户户忙着贴春联、挂红灯笼、包饺子、做年夜饭，孩子们忙着放鞭炮。春节及之后的几天，全家人会一起走亲访友，互赠礼物。孩子们要给长辈们拜年，长辈会给孩子们压岁钱。

贴春联

拜年

互赠礼物

跟着妮妮学一学
Learning Chinese calligraphy with Nini

篆书 (zhuan shu) | Seal script

“立”字的本义是“站立”。篆书“立”的字形像一个人分开两腿，站立在地上。

“立” means “to stand”. The seal script of “立” resembles a man standing straight on the ground with his legs apart.

篆书“春”字是由“日”、“木”和“屯”组成的。它的字形像草木的嫩芽，意指在太阳的照耀下，草木萌发，春天到来。

The seal script of “春” consists of “日”、“木”and “屯”. Its image resembles the scenario where grass and trees bloom in the sunshine when spring comes.

跟着杰瑞写一写

Practicing calligraphy with Jerry

楷书（kai shu）| Regular script

在学写"立春"之前，我们先来学习书法中一些常见的基本笔画。之后大家可以举一反三进行练习。

Before we start writing "立春", let's learn some fundamental strokes in Chinese calligraphy first. Then you will be able to apply them to your later practice.

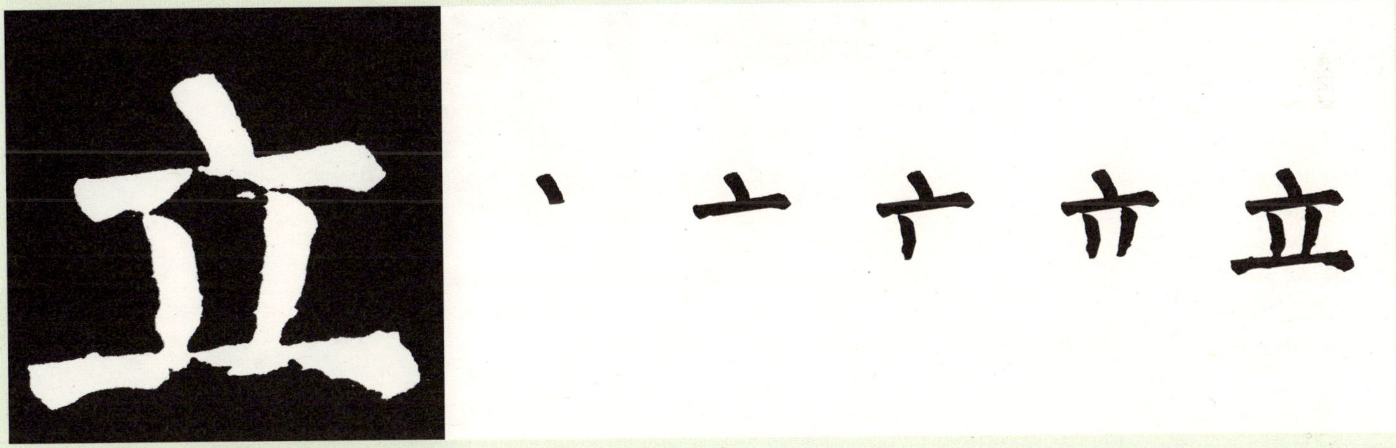

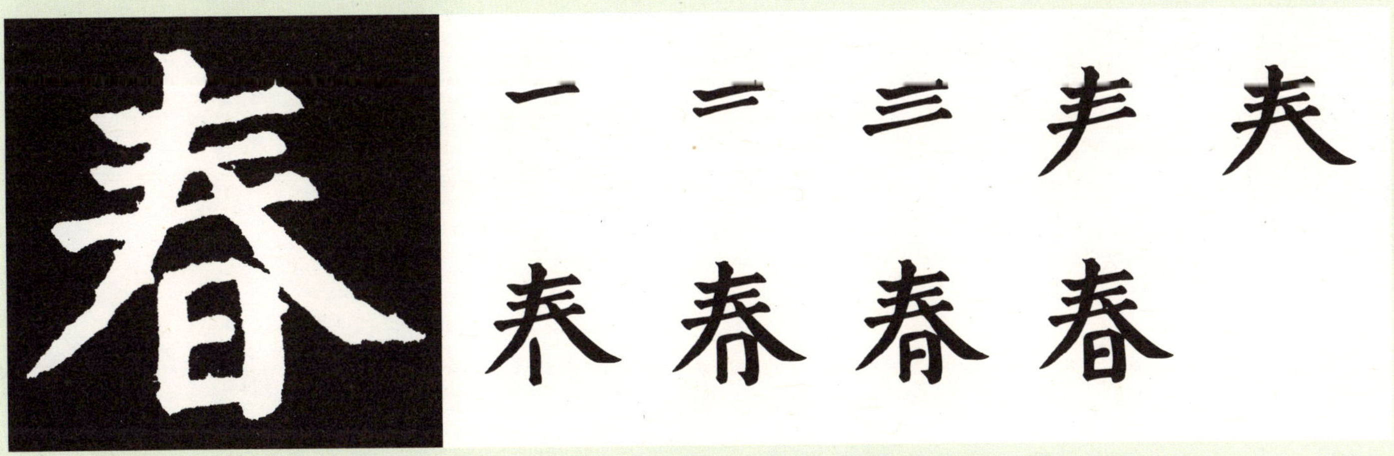

做立春的礼物

Make a gift with Chinese characters "立春"

跟着妮妮和杰瑞做送给朋友的礼物

Let's make some gifts for our friends with Nini and Jerry

剪一剪、画一画

Paper cutting and graphic design

妮妮的剪纸

paper cutting by Nini

杰瑞的画

graphic designed by Jerry

猜一猜、说一说

Let's make a guess

与妮妮和杰瑞一起猜一猜

Let's make a guess with Nini and Jerry

与“立春”对应的是哪个星座？

Which astrological sign corresponds to Beginning of Spring?

与妮妮和杰瑞一起比赛

Let's have a competition with Nini and Jerry

说出与“春”有关的词语

Try to say as many words as you can that are relevant to “春”

妮妮，最近几天细雨绵绵，河面的冰都已经融化，又要开始新的节气了吗？

Hi Nini, it has been drizzling in recent days and the icy river has thawed out. Is there a new solar term around the corner?

杰瑞，你说的没错，中国有句古话叫作“立春天渐暖，雨水送肥忙”。立春之后的下一个节气就是雨水。

Yes, Jerry, you are right. An old Chinese saying has it that the weather starts to get warmer after Beginning of Spring, and farmers start to get busier with fertilizing the soil after Rain Water. The solar term after Beginning of Spring is Rain Water.

雨水

Rain Water

Yu Shui

The story of

Rain Water

Important facts about Rain Water

Rain Water comes between 18th and 20th February. From the point of Rain Water, weather starts to get warmer and rainfall starts to increase. Plants sprout and farmers start to fertilize their fields.

Changes after Rain Water

Plants resurge. Swan geese migrate to the north.

Willows sprout. Apricot trees come into blossom.

Icy ponds thaw out. Otters start fishing.

雨水大事记

雨水的时间点是在每年的2月18～20日之间。从雨水开始，天气渐渐变暖，下雨天逐渐增多，植物开始抽芽生长，农民伯伯开始往田地里施肥。

雨水变化

草木萌动，鸿雁北飞。
柳树发芽，杏花开放。
池塘解冻，水獭捕鱼。

the Lantern Festival

The 14th day after the Spring Festival is the Lantern Festival, which is 15th January on the Chinese lunar calendar. It has the first full moon of the year. In the evening, Chinese people have sweet dumplings while they are appreciating the moon. Other entertainment includes firing fireworks with friends, having a tour around the night fair of lanterns and guessing the riddles written on lanterns. The Spring Festival holiday comes to an end after the Lantern Festival.

eat sweet dumplings

walk around with a lantern shaped in a rabbit

guess the riddles written on lanterns

元宵节

春节后的第十四天，即农历正月十五，就是中国的传统节日元宵节。这一天是一年中首个月圆之夜，晚上人们会在赏月的同时品尝元宵节的传统食物——元宵，还会结伴放烟花、赏花灯，猜灯谜。过了元宵节，才算真正过完年。

吃元宵

遛兔子灯

猜灯谜

篆书 (zhuan shu) | Seal script

“雨”字的本义是雨水，它的篆书字形像从天空落下阵阵水滴。

“雨” originally means rain. The seal script of “雨” resembles rainfall from the sky.

“水”字的本义是水流，它的篆书字形像水流动的样子。

“水” originally means water. The seal script of “水” resembles water flow.

跟着杰瑞写一写

Practicing calligraphy with Jerry

楷书 (kai shu) | Regular script

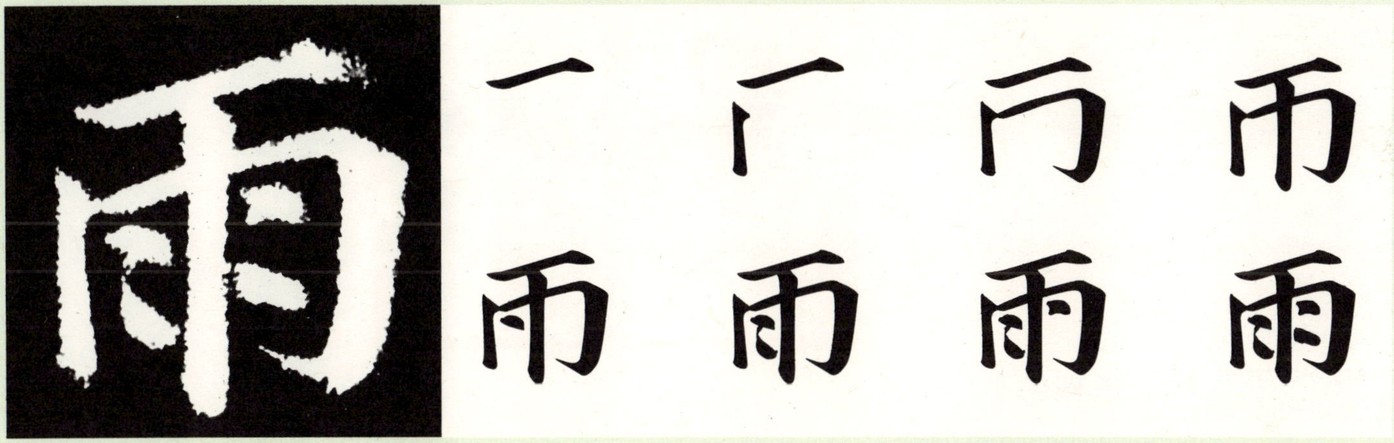

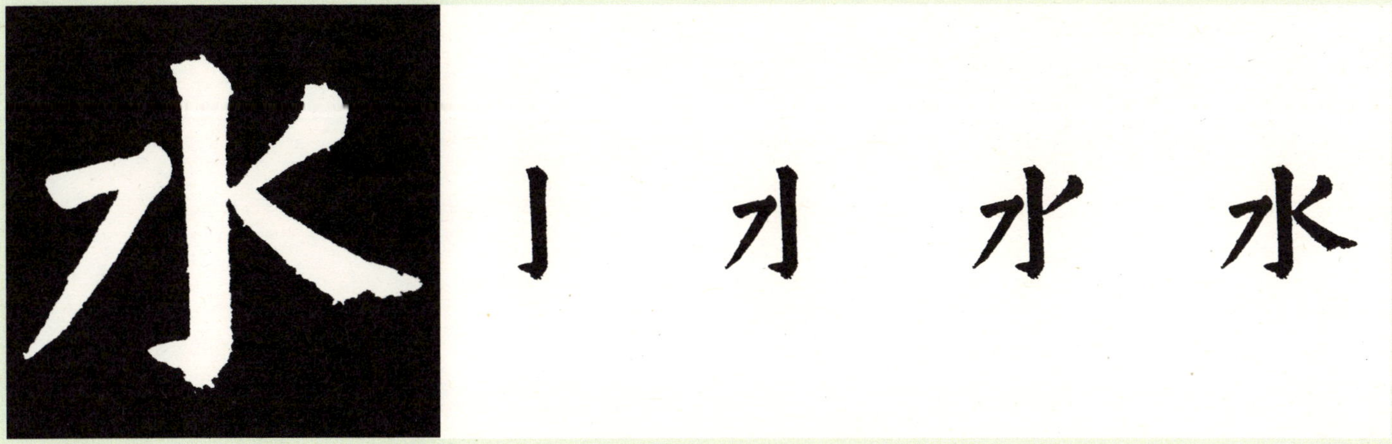

剪一剪、画一画

Paper cutting and graphic design

做雨水的礼物

Make a gift with Chinese characters "雨水"

跟着妮妮和杰瑞做送给朋友的礼物

Let's make some gifts for our friends with Nini and Jerry

妮妮的剪纸

paper cutting by Nini

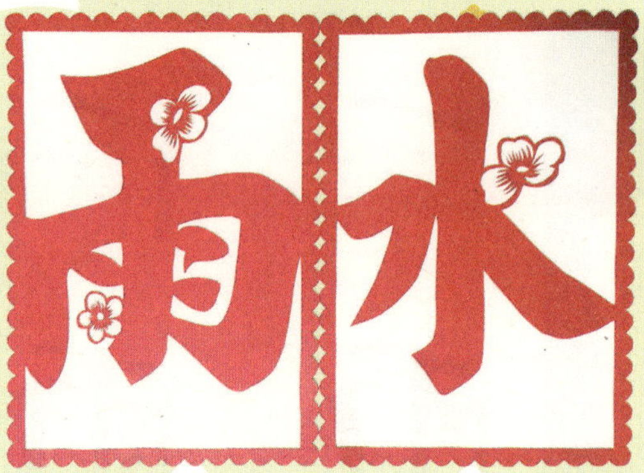

杰瑞的画

graphic designed by Jerry

猜一猜、说一说

Let's make a guess

与妮妮和杰瑞一起猜一猜

Let's make a guess with Nini and Jerry

与“雨水”对应
的是哪个星座？

Which astrological sign corresponds
to the Rain Water?

与妮妮和杰瑞一起比赛

Let's have a competition with Nini and Jerry

说出与“雨”
有关的词语

Try to say as many words as you can
that are relevant to “雨”

惊蛰

Insects Awakening
Jing Zhe

The story of **Insects Awakening**

Important facts about Insects Awakening

Insects Awakening, "Jing Zhe" in Chinese, comes on 5th or 6th March every year. "Jing" means to disturb. "Zhe" means to hide. On the day of Insects Awakening, the thunder in spring would wake up the hibernating animals and insects.

Changes after Insects Awakening

Temperature keeps rising. The ground has thawed.
Peach trees come into blossom. Orioles start to tweet.
Thunder starts to rumble. Animals wake up from hibernation.

惊蛰大事记

惊蛰的时间点是在每年的3月5～7日之间。"惊"即惊动，"蛰"为藏之意，所谓"惊蛰"就是春雷的响声把冬眠的动物和蛰伏在地下的昆虫给惊醒了。

惊蛰变化

气温回升，土壤解冻。
桃花盛开，黄鹂鸣叫。
春雷始鸣，动物苏醒。

篆书（zhuan shu）| Seal script

篆书"驚"字为"惊"的繁体字，是上声下形，由"敬"和"马"(繁体)两部分组成。"驚"指马受惊。

The seal script of "驚" is the traditional complex form of the simplified character "惊". It is composed of two characters — "敬"and "马" — with the upper part standing for the sound while the bottom part stands for the meaning. The whole character literally means that a horse got startled.

"蛰"字为动物隐藏冬眠之意，是上声下形，由"执"和"虫"两个部件组成。

"蛰"refers to animals hibernating in their dens. The upper part "执" stands for the sound and the bottom part "虫" stands for the meaning.

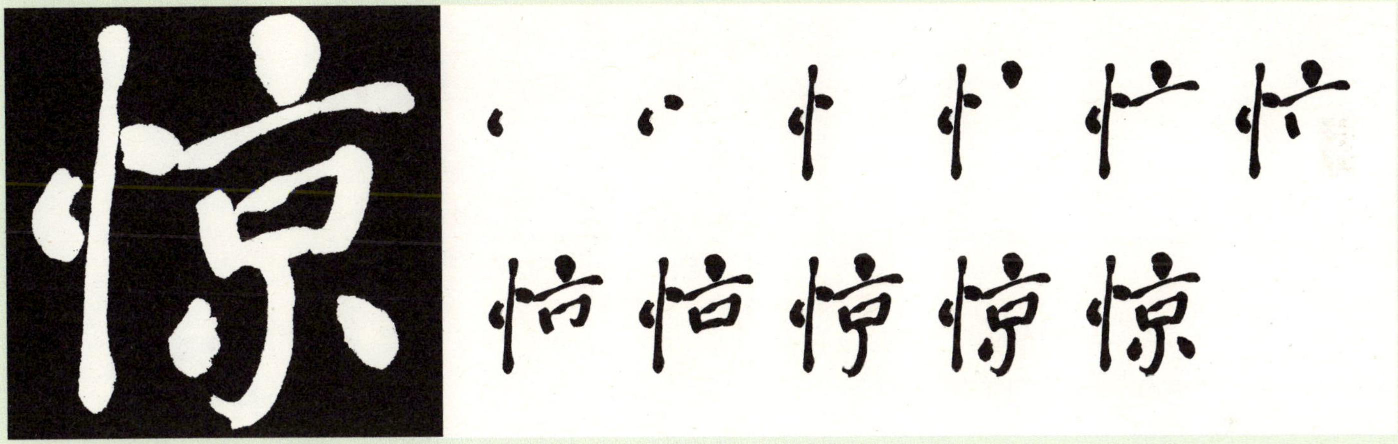

惊

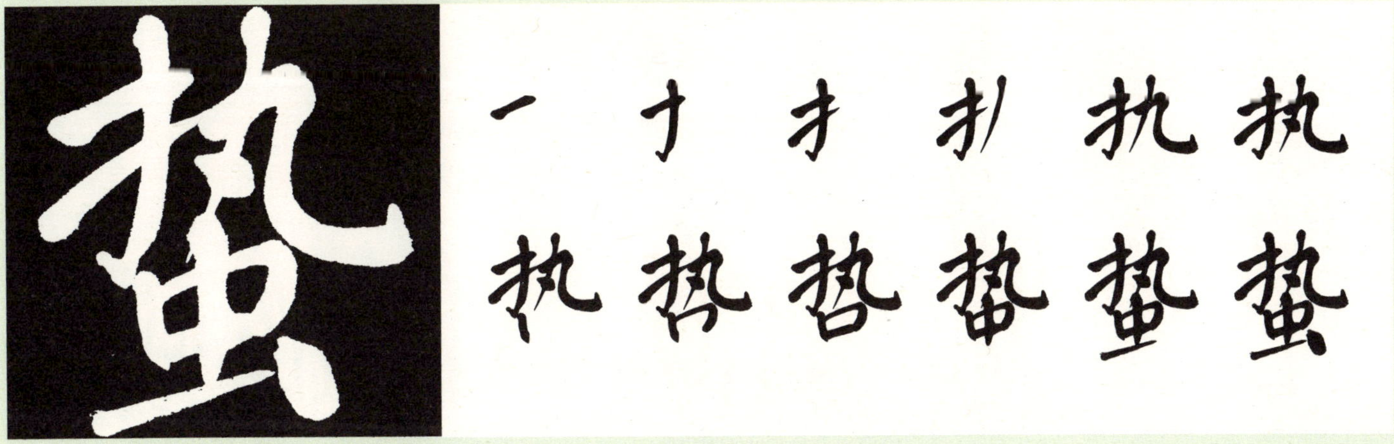

蛰

剪一剪、画一画

Paper cutting and graphic design

做惊蛰的礼物

Make a gift with Chinese characters “惊蛰”

跟着妮妮和杰瑞
做送给朋友的
礼物

Let’s make some gifts for our friends with Nini and Jerry

妮妮的剪纸

paper cutting by Nini

杰瑞的画

graphic designed by Jerry

猜一猜、说一说

Let's make a guess

与妮妮和杰瑞一起猜一猜

Let's make a guess with Nini and Jerry

与惊蛰对应的是
哪个星座？

Which astrological sign corresponds
to Insects Awakening?

与妮妮和杰瑞一起比赛

Let's have a competition with Nini and Jerry

说出与"惊"
有关的词语

Try to say as many words as you can
that are relevant to "惊"

春分

Spring Equinox
Chun Fen

The story of

Spring Equinox

Important facts about Spring Equinox

Spring Equinox, "Chun Fen" in Chinese, comes between 20th and 21st March every year. "Fen" means to be equally divided. When Spring Equinox arrives, half of the spring has passed. Spring Equinox is the day when the day time equals the night time in both north and south hemispheres. After Spring Equinox, the daytime in northern hemisphere starts to get longer and longer, while the nights start to get shorter and shorter.

Changes after Spring Equinox

Begonias bloom. Grass flourishes and warblers swiftly fly.
Swallows return from the south. People start to fly kites for entertainment.
Thunder storms arise. Farmers start to plough their fields and become busier.

春分大事记

春分的时间点是在每年的3月20～21日之间。“分”即平分，是指到了春分这一天，春季就过了一半。而且在这一天，南北半球的白天和夜晚时间一样长，之后北半球的白天会越来越长，夜晚会越来越短。

春分变化

海棠花开，草长莺飞。
燕子归来，放飞纸鸢。
雷乃发声，春耕农忙。

小贴士 纸鸢：即风筝。

篆书 (zhuan shu) | Seal script

篆书"春"字是由"日"、"木"和"屯"组成的。它的字形像草木的嫩芽，意指在太阳的照耀下，草木萌发，春天到来。

The seal script of "春" consists of "日"、"木" and "屯". Its image resembles the scenario where grass and trees bloom in the sunshine when spring comes.

"分"，切开之意。按图所示，在"刀"部的左右各有一笔，表示执刀将物体切分成两部分。

"分" means to cut open. As is showed in the seal script of "刀",there is a stroke on both sides, which means to cut something from the middle.

跟着杰瑞写一写
Practicing calligraphy with Jerry

楷书 (kai shu) | Regular script

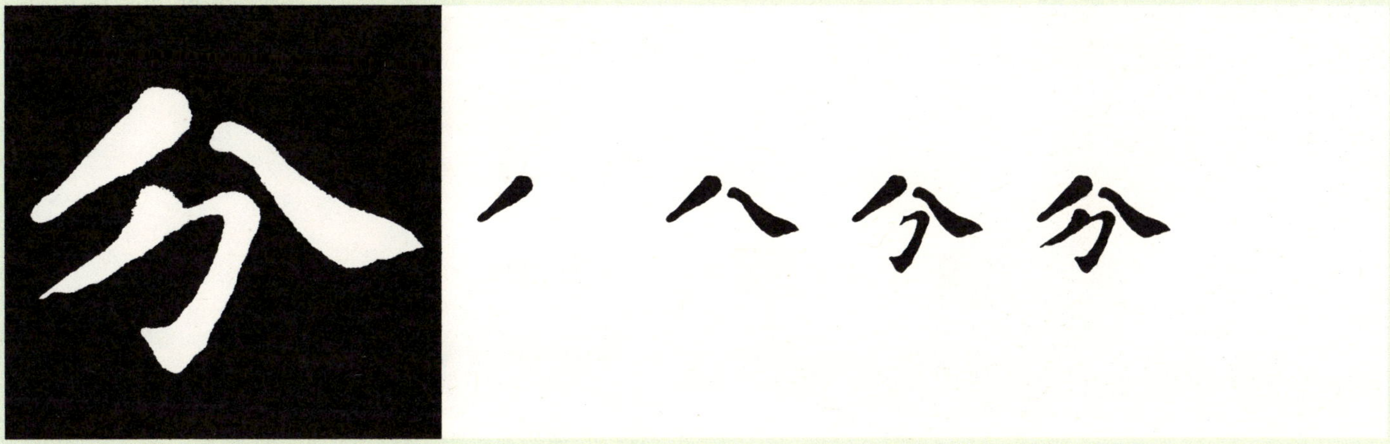

做春分的礼物

Make a gift with Chinese characters “春分”

跟着妮妮和杰瑞做送给朋友的礼物

Let’s make some gifts for our friends with Nini and Jerry

剪一剪、画一画

Paper cutting and graphic design

妮妮的剪纸

paper cutting by Nini

杰瑞的画

graphic designed by Jerry

猜一猜、说一说

Let's make a guess

与妮妮和杰瑞一起猜一猜

Let's make a guess with Nini and Jerry

与“春分”对应的是哪个星座？

Which astrological sign corresponds to Spring Equinox?

与妮妮和杰瑞一起比赛

Let's have a competition with Nini and Jerry

说出与“分”有关的词语

Try to say as many words as you can that are relevant to “分”

清明

Fresh Green
Qing Ming

The story of **Fresh Green**

Important facts about Fresh Green

Fresh Green comes between 4th and 6th April every year. At that time, the air is fresh and the scenery is bright and beautiful. Spring reaches its peak where it is perfect for planting crops. An old Chinese saying has it that it is the best time to plant gourds and legumes around Fresh Green. Fresh Green is not only a solar term, but also a day for Chinese people to mourn for their ancestors, called Qingming Festival.

Changes after Fresh Green

Tung flowers come into full blossom. Rainbow has its debut.

People go for a walk in the countryside. It is also the time to plant willow trees and sweep our ancestors' tombs.

People plant trees as well as gourds and legumes.

eating sweet green dumplings

清明的故事

清明大事记

清明的时间点是在每年的4月4～6日之间。清明时节，气清景明，春意正浓，是春耕的好时节。中国有一句古话叫作：“清明前后，种瓜点豆。”清明不仅是节气，也是中国人祭祀祖先、缅怀先人的传统节日。

清明变化

桐花盛放，彩虹始现。
踏青寻春，插柳扫墓。
植树造林，种瓜点豆。

吃青团

跟着妮妮学一学
Learning Chinese calligraphy with Nini

篆书 (zhuan shu) | Seal script

“清”字由“水”和“青”组合而成，左形右声。“青”音同“清”字，“水”意指水清透澄澈的样子。

Character“清” consists of the left-hand “水”,which stands for the meaning, and the right-hand “青”, which stands for the pronunciation. “青” has the same pronunciation as “清” does. The left-hand “水” means crystal water.

“明”字由“日”和“月”组合而成，表示日月照耀，有光明之意。

“明” is composed of “日” and “月”. It means the sun and the moon shine, making the world bright.

小贴士

“明”为典型的会意字。它的字体曾有三种形式：朙、眀和明。“朙”由月和一个窗形结构组成，意思是月光照进窗内，表示光亮之意；“眀”由目和月两个部件组成，表示眼睛看到了月光，有明亮之意；“明”由日和月两个部件组成，表示日月交替照耀，即光明之意。

楷书 (kai shu) | Regular script

清

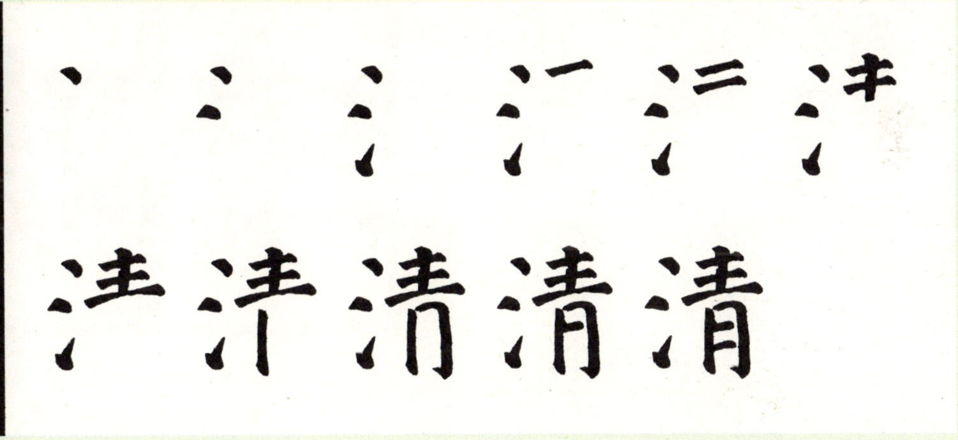

明

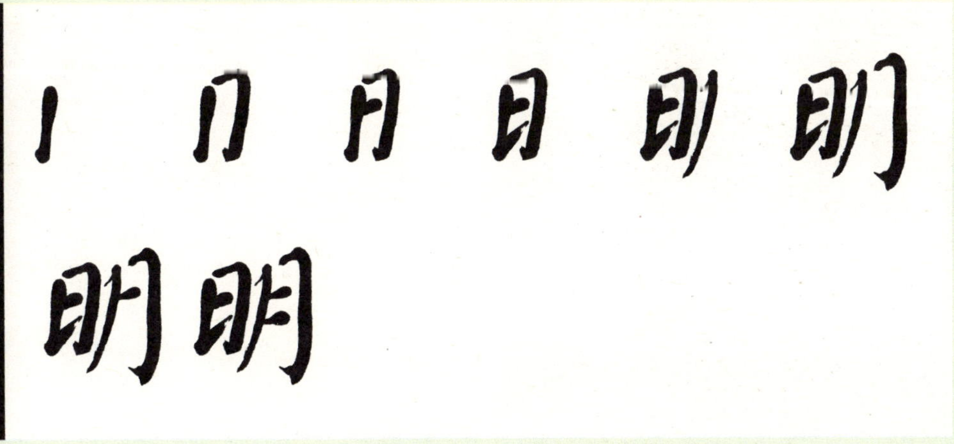

剪一剪、画一画

Paper cutting and graphic design

做清明的礼物

Make a gift with Chinese characters "清明"

跟着妮妮和杰瑞做送给朋友的礼物

Let's make some gifts for our friends with Nini and Jerry

妮妮的剪纸

paper cutting by Nini

杰瑞的画

graphic designed by Jerry

猜一猜、说一说

Let's make a guess

与妮妮和杰瑞一起猜一猜

Let's make a guess with Nini and Jerry

与"清明"对应的是哪个星座？

Which astrological sign corresponds to Fresh Green?

与妮妮和杰瑞一起比赛

Let's have a competition with Nini and Jerry

说出与"清"有关的词语

Try to say as many words as you can that are relevant to "清"

谷雨

Grain Rain
Gu Yu

The story of **Grain Rain**

Important facts about Grain Rain

Grain Rain, which is the last solar term in spring, comes between 19th and 21st April. The name of Grain Rain comes from the old saying "Rain nurtures all kinds of grain". Between Grain Rain and the end of spring, the rise in temperature accelerates and rainfall increases, which is quite beneficial to the growth of crops.

Changes after Grain Rain

- Rainfall increases. Temperature rises.
- Cuckoos sing. Peonies bloom.
- People start to sow their field with seeds and transfer the sprouts.
- Silkworms spin.

谷雨大事记

谷雨是春季最后一个节气，时间点是在每年的4月19～21日之间。谷雨取自“雨生百谷”的说法。这一时节，气温回暖加快，雨水明显增多，十分利于农作物的播种、生长。

谷雨变化

雨水增多，气温回暖。
布谷鸟叫，牡丹花开。
播种移苗，春蚕吐丝。

跟着妮妮学一学
Learning Chinese calligraphy with Nini

篆书 (zhuan shu) | Seal script

"谷"字由上下两部分组成，它的上半部分像溪流，下半部分像出口，意思是两山间狭长而有出口的水道。

"谷" is composed of an upper part which resembles a brook and a bottom part which resembles an estuary. It means a long and narrow water channel between mountains with an estuary.

"雨"字的本义是雨水，它的篆书字形像从天空落下阵阵水滴。

"雨" originally means rainfall. The seal script of "雨" resembles raindrops falling from the sky.

楷书 (kai shu) | Regular script

剪一剪、画一画

Paper cutting and graphic design

做谷雨的礼物

Make a gift with Chinese characters "谷雨"

跟着妮妮和杰瑞做送给朋友的礼物

Let's make some gifts for our friends with Nini and Jerry

妮妮的剪纸

paper cutting by Nini

杰瑞的画

graphic designed by Jerry

猜一猜、说一说

Let's make a guess

与妮妮和杰瑞一起猜一猜

Let's make a guess with Nini and Jerry

与"谷雨"对应
的是哪个星座？

Which astrological sign corresponds
with Grain Rain?

与妮妮和杰瑞一起比赛

Let's have a competition with Nini and Jerry

说出与"谷"
有关的词语

Try to say as many words as you can
that are relevant to "谷"

后记

自2014年完成了“书法小联合国”文化特色教材《十二生肖我来写》之后，一直收到不同国家各级学校老师发来的邮件，询问是否可以买到课程的示范录像，也有老师与家长鼓励我继续编写一些有趣的关于中国传统文化的书法教材。

编写海外书法文化启蒙教材是一件十分艰难的事，看起来只是一本几十页的小书，要编写好绝非一日之功。首先要找到一个好的素材，之后要在不同的文化语境中反复进行教学实验，咨询各方专家的意见，最后方能定稿。多年来，“书法小联合国”国际系列教材编写的目标是：教材既要遵循受众国的文化习俗，又要在编写上做到准确、有趣，把中国故事讲好。

《风调雨顺：春夏秋冬》四册书法文化启蒙教材从酝酿到动笔撰写就花了近五年的时间，教材主要实验地在北美与南美部分学校，实验教材在使用过程中受到学生与教师的欢迎。该教材一方面介绍中国古代气象文化，以故事主人公中国妮妮给美国杰瑞讲故事的方式展开情节；另一方面，通过讲解汉字的构字特点来帮助不同文化背景的学生认知汉字里的文化，并采用二维码形式附上书法教学视频，方便实用，帮助学习者在书法、绘画、剪纸等艺术形式中加强对中国文化的整体理解。

感谢前联合国秘书长潘基文先生、上海交通大学张伟民教授、美国理海大学康妮教授、纽约大学唐力行教授、联合国国际学校孙青倩等老师在该教材编写过程中提出的中肯建议。感谢华东师范大学出版社王焰社长在教材出版过程中的大力支持。相信这四册“书法小联合国”汉字书法文化系列教材的顺利出版，会在中国书法文化国际教材开发中发挥积极的示范作用。

周斌于中国书法文化国际传播研究所
2017年10月28日

Postscript

Since the publication of *Let Me Write the Twelve Zodiac Signs* which belongs to the special course on calligraphy culture by United Association of Calligraphy in 2014, I have been receiving mails from parents and teachers from different schools all over the world. They asked me whether they could buy the video recordings of some demo lessons. And some of them encouraged me to keep writing more interesting calligraphy course books relevant to traditional Chinese culture.

It is not an easy task to compile a course book on calligraphy culture for overseas learners. Just as Rome was not built in a day, such a thin book of tens of pages also cannot be completed within a day. First of all, we need to find a suitable topic and its relevant materials. Then, we need to test the course book through continuous classroom instructions in various cultural contexts. After that we consult experts from all walks of life, and with feedback from classrooms, we finally make the decision to mass produce the course book. Our international course book series aim not only to suit the customs of the overseas learners but also to tell the stories of Chinese culture with accuracy and amusement.

From the blueprint to the first draft of the four course books — *Spring/Summer/Fall/Winter: Season with Timely Breeze and Rain for Crop Raising* — for the enlightenment on Chinese calligraphy culture, it took us nearly five years to present them to the public. These course books were put on trial mainly in some schools in North and South America and got very positive feedback from both teachers and students. This course book series introduces Chinese people's understanding of the climate in ancient time through stories told by a Chinese character named Nini to an American character named Jerry. Furthermore, we have selected some ancient Chinese characters to help students from different cultural backgrounds get a better appreciation of the culture of Chinese characters. Moreover, we have attached a QR code in the part Practicing Calligraphy with Jerry. If you scan the QR code, you can watch videos teaching you how to write the characters. Learners' comprehensive understanding of Chinese culture will be improved by learning and practicing Chinese calligraphy.

Here I want to extend my sincere gratitude to the former UN Secretary-General, Mr Ban Ki-moon; Professor Zhang Weimin from Shanghai Jiao Tong University, Professor Connie from Lehigh University, and Professor Lixing Tang from New York University for their pertinent suggestions during the process of compiling these course books. I'm also grateful to president of East China Normal University Press, Mrs Yan Wang, for her substantial support during the publication process. I firmly believe that the publication of these four course books would play a very positive role in the development of international course books on Chinese calligraphy culture.

Zhou Bin

In Chinese Calligraphy Culture Education and Communication Center

28th October 2017

图书在版编目（CIP）数据

风调雨顺. 春 / 周斌，周佳楠主编. —上海：华东师范大学出版社，2018
ISBN 978-7-5675-7398-7

Ⅰ. ①风… Ⅱ. ①周… ②周… Ⅲ. ①汉语－对外汉语教学－语言读物 Ⅳ. ① H195.5

中国版本图书馆 CIP 数据核字（2018）第 006653 号

风调雨顺 · 春

主　　编　周　斌　周佳楠
策划编辑　王　焰
责任编辑　曹　琛
责任校对　时东明
封面设计　刘怡霖

出版发行　华东师范大学出版社
社　　址　上海市中山北路 3663 号　邮编 200062
网　　址　www.ecnupress.com.cn
电　　话　021-60821666　行政传真　021-62572105
客服电话　021-62865537　门市（邮购）电话　021-62869887
地　　址　上海市中山北路 3663 号华东师范大学校内先锋路口
网　　店　http://hdsdcbs.tmall.com

印 刷 者　上海盛通时代印刷有限公司
开　　本　700×1000　12 开
印　　张　7⅔
字　　数　60 千字
版　　次　2018 年 3 月第 1 版
印　　次　2018 年 8 月第 2 次
书　　号　ISBN 978-7-5675-7398-7/G · 10888
定　　价　48.00 元
出 版 人　王　焰

（如发现本版图书有印订质量问题，请寄回本社客服中心调换或电话 021-62865537 联系）

练习册使用说明

本书为《风调雨顺 · 春》教材的配套练习册，希望通过二十四节气相关汉字的书法练习，使读者掌握书法学习的要领。本练习册通过对汉字字体笔顺和笔画的分析，为学习者掌握汉字的书写方法提供指导。同时，描红及空格练习也便于读者对照示范汉字进行反复书写。

This is the workbook for our course book *Spring: Season with Timely Breeze and Rain for Crop Raising*. We hope that readers will be able to master the principles of writing Chinese calligraphy after practicing the Chinese characters relevant to the Twenty-four Solar Terms. This workbook is going to give a detailed demonstration on strokes and the organization of these strokes in our sample characters, so as to provide a guidance of writing Chinese calligraphy for our learners. At the same time, the particular framework we offer in this workbook for learners to write in is very helpful because learners can practice repeatedly by imitating.

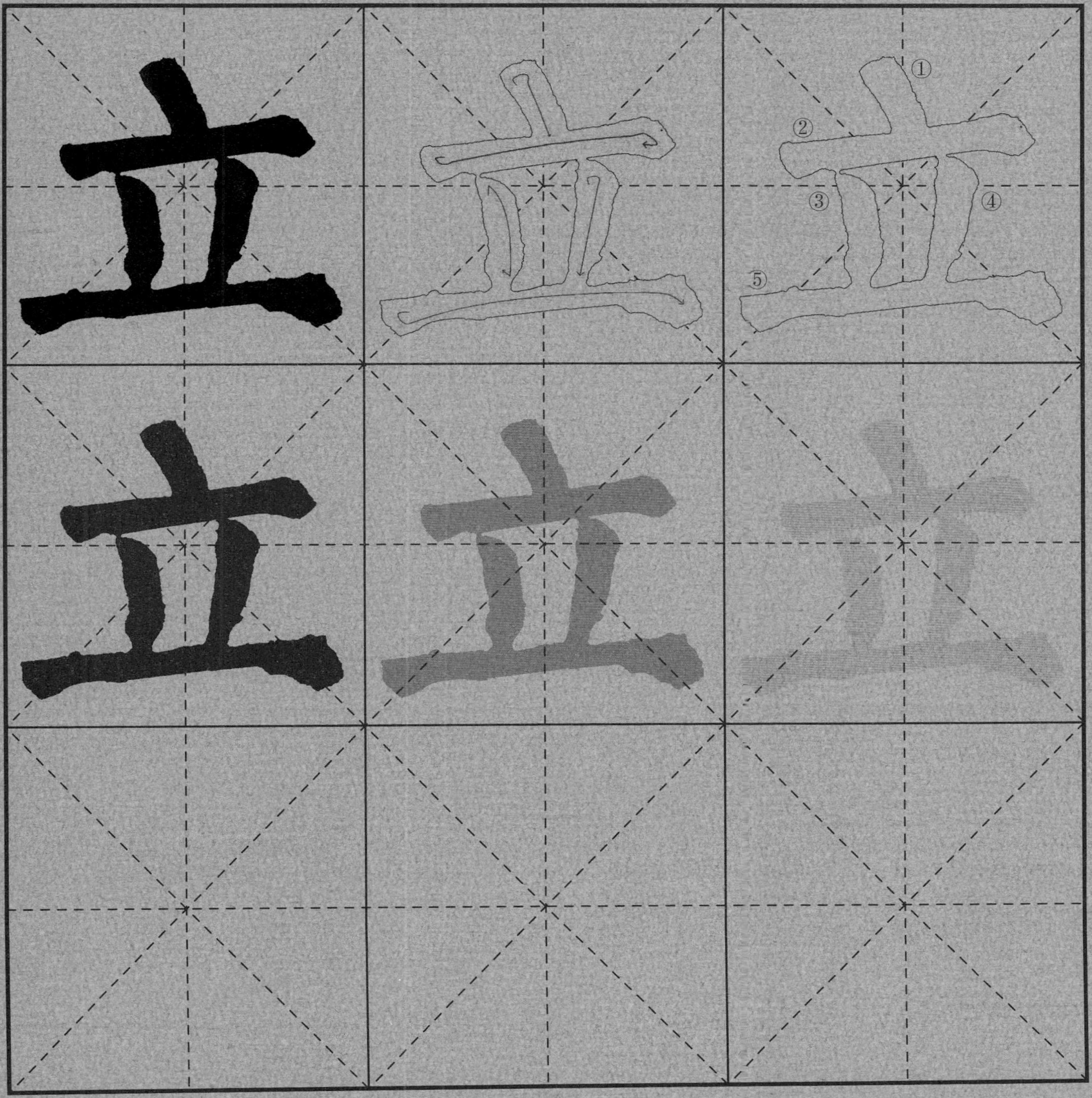
立
①
②
③
④
⑤

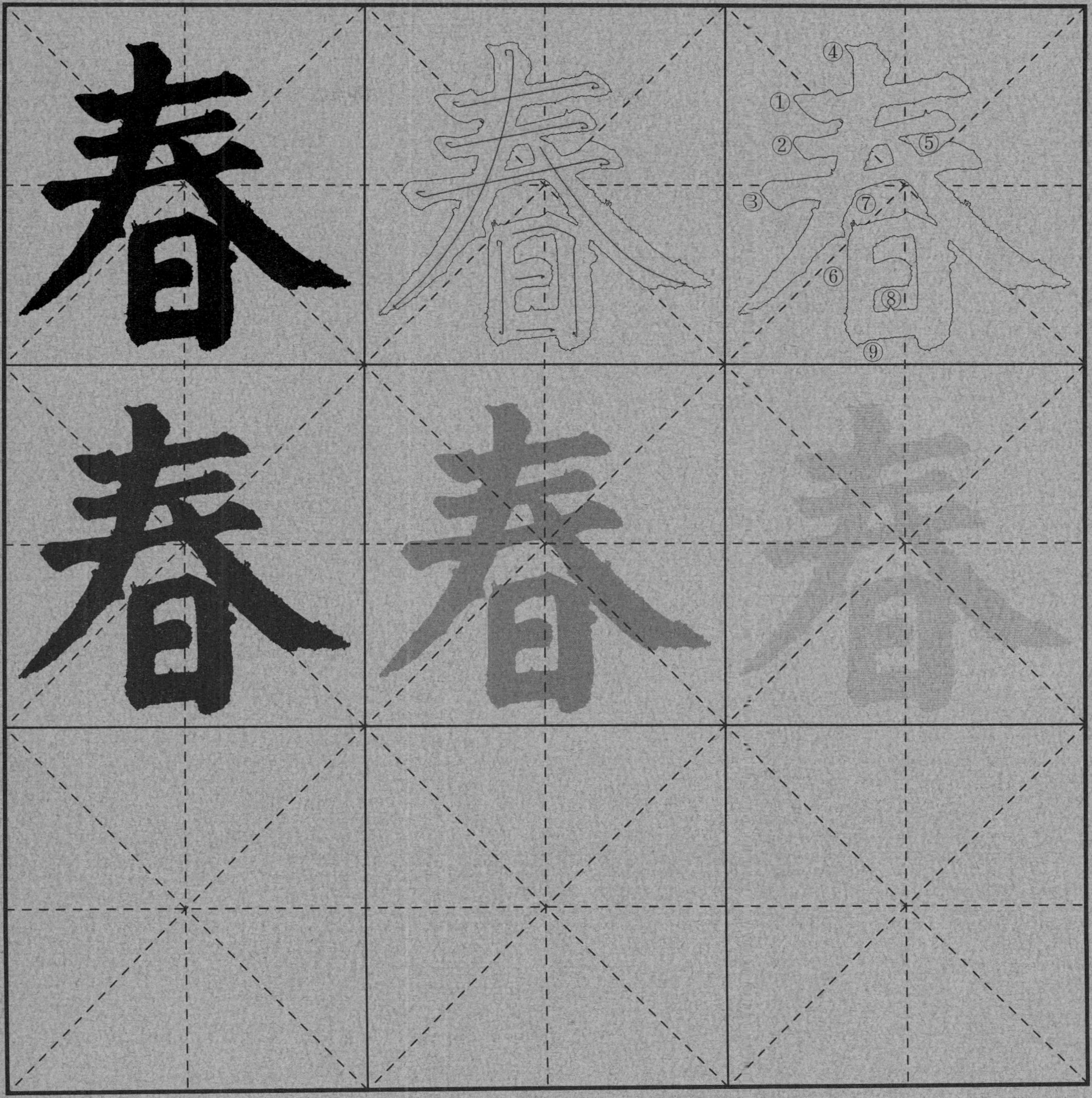

春
①
②
③
④
⑤
⑥
⑦
⑧
⑨

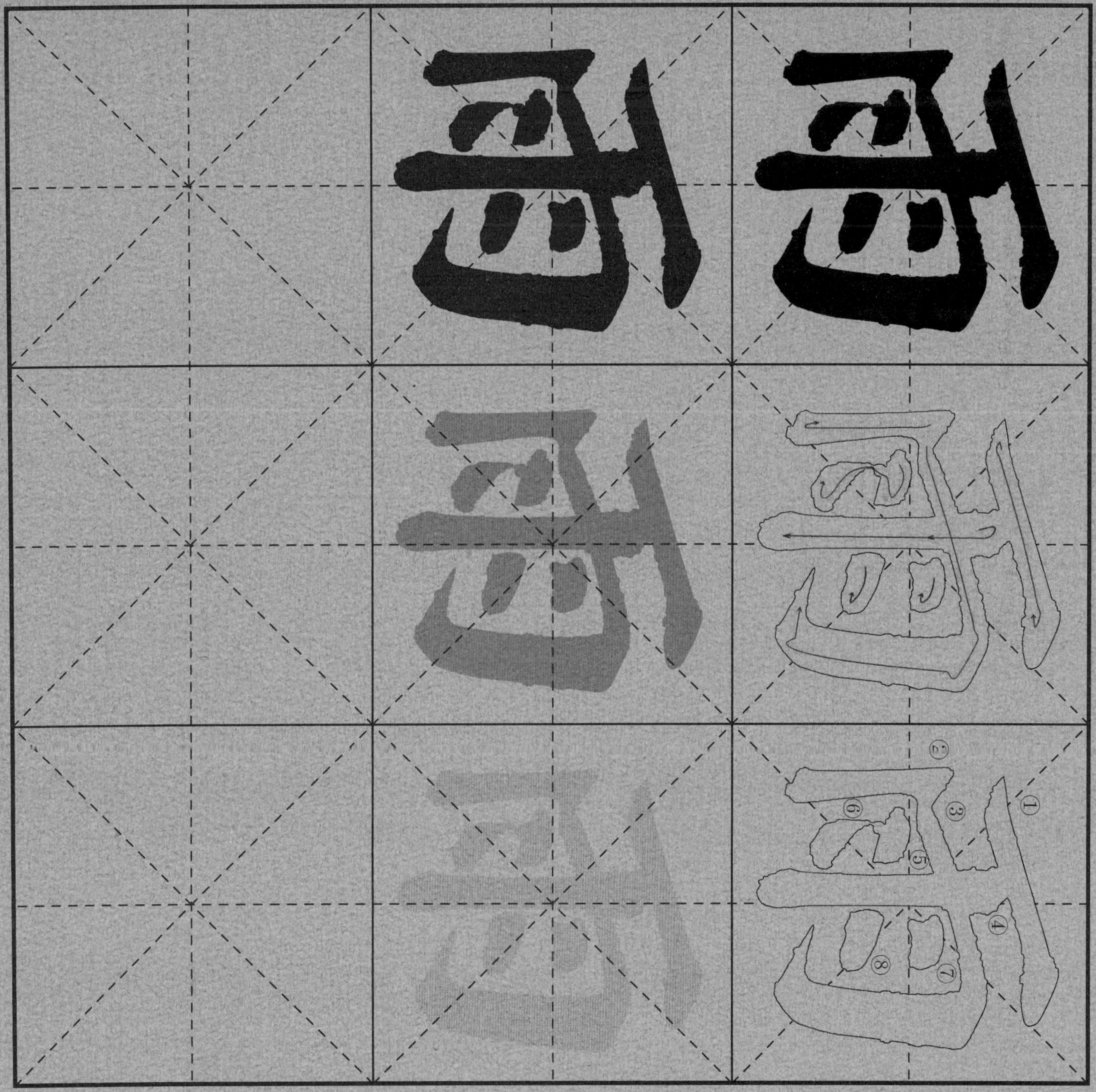
哥

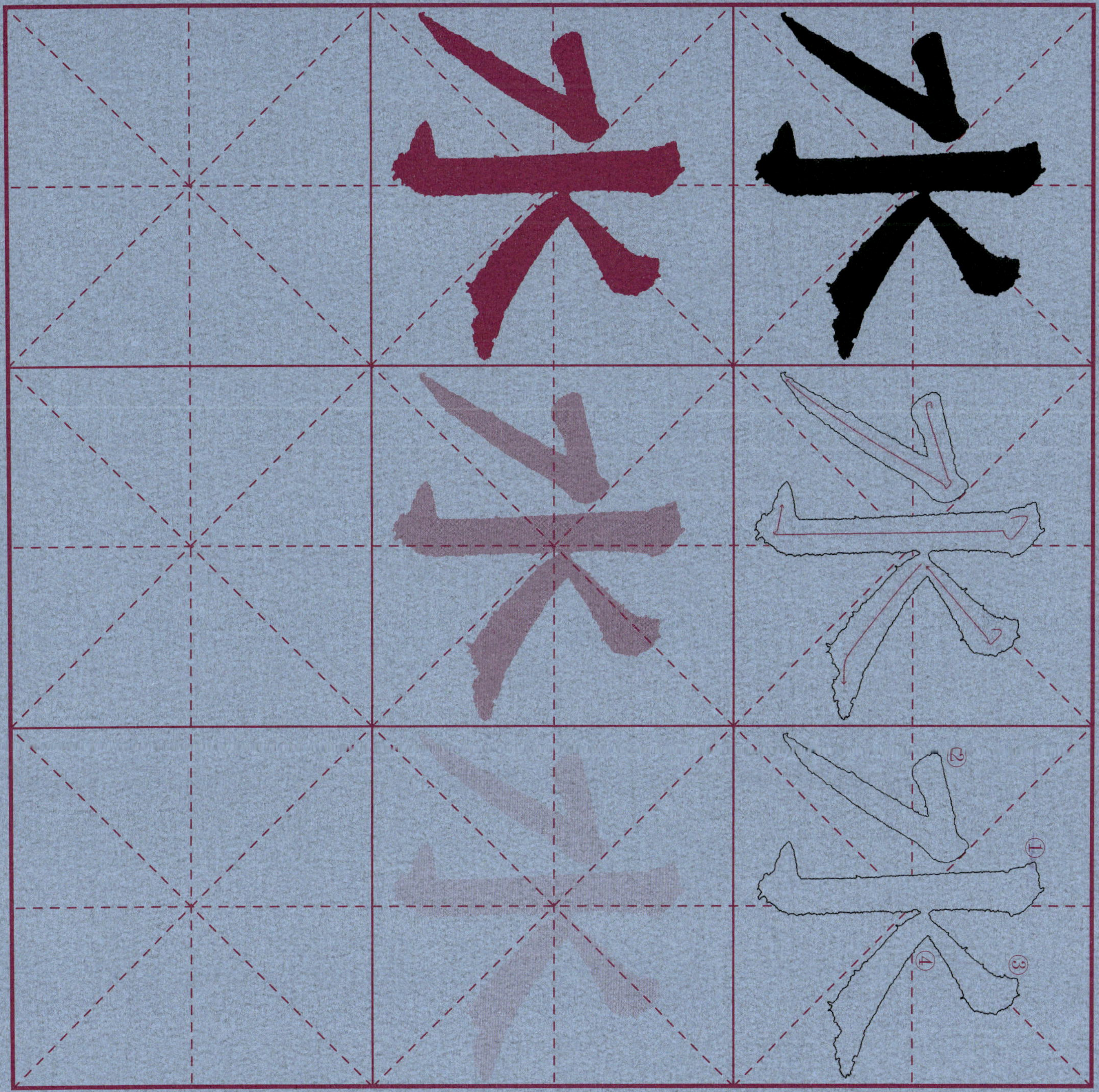
①
②
③
④

①
③
②
⑩
⑧
⑥
⑤
⑦
⑨
④
⑪

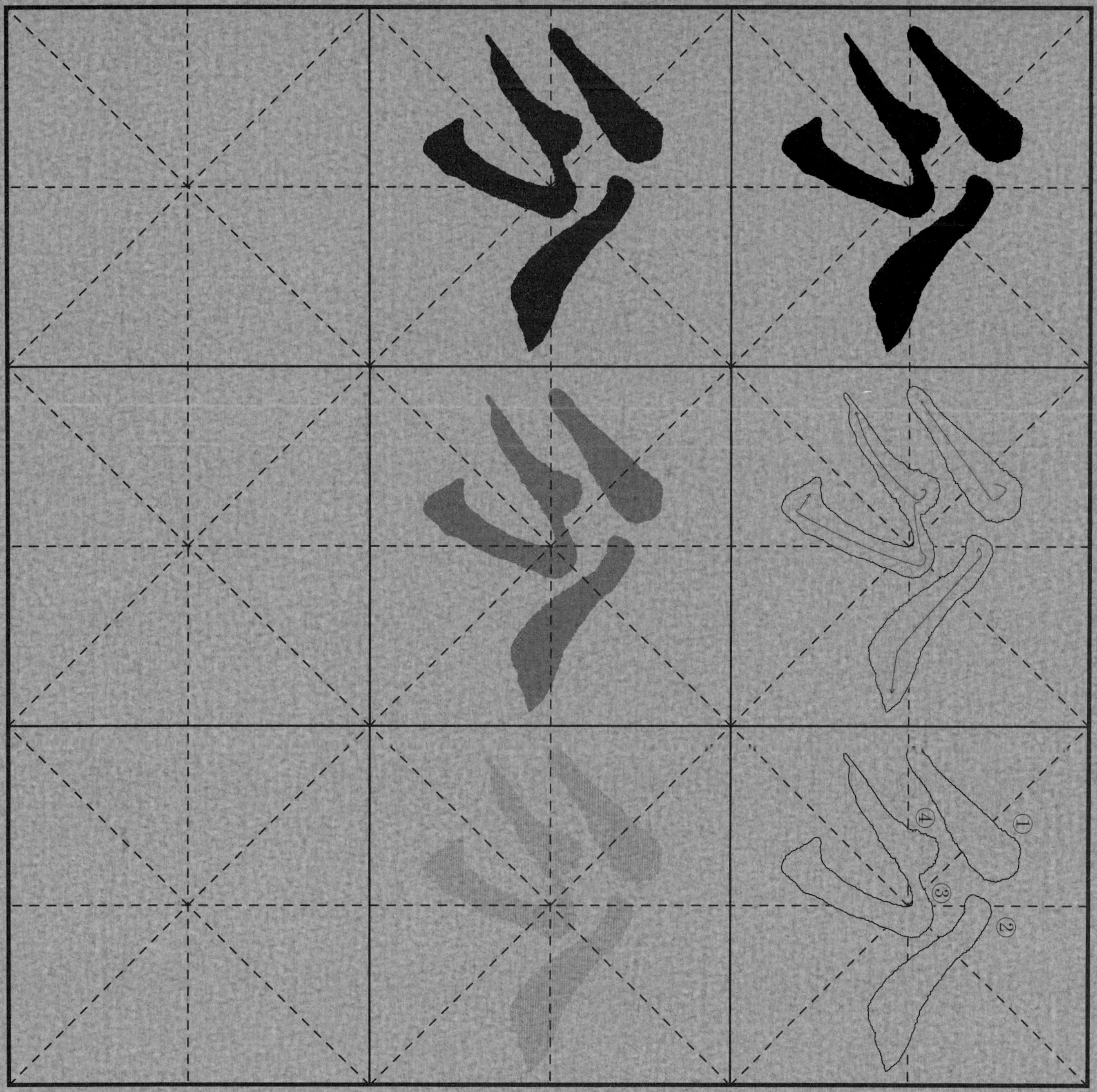
①
②
③
④

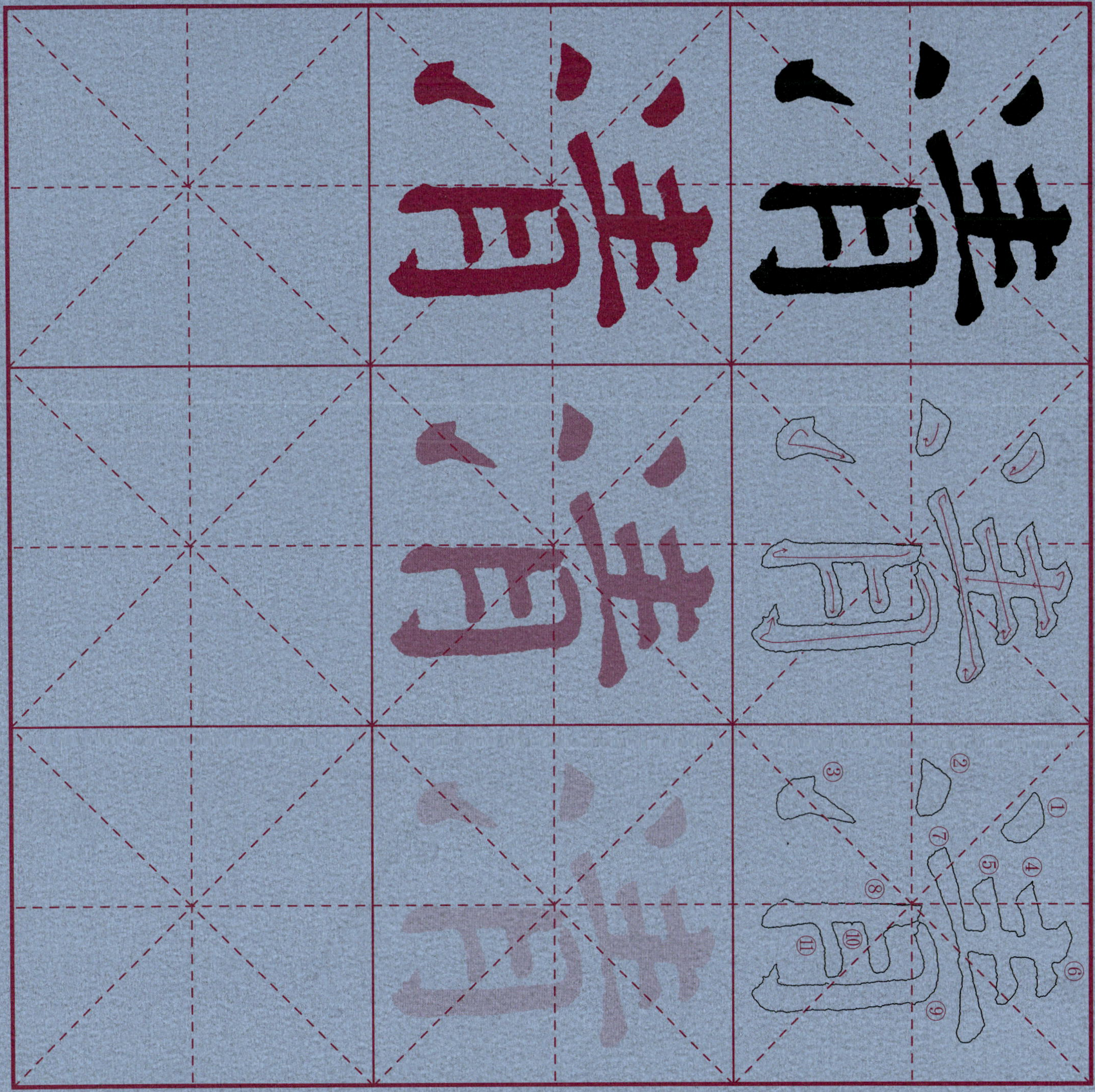
清
① ② ③ ④ ⑤ ⑥ ⑦ ⑧ ⑨ ⑩ ⑪

①
②
③
④
⑤
⑥
⑦
⑧

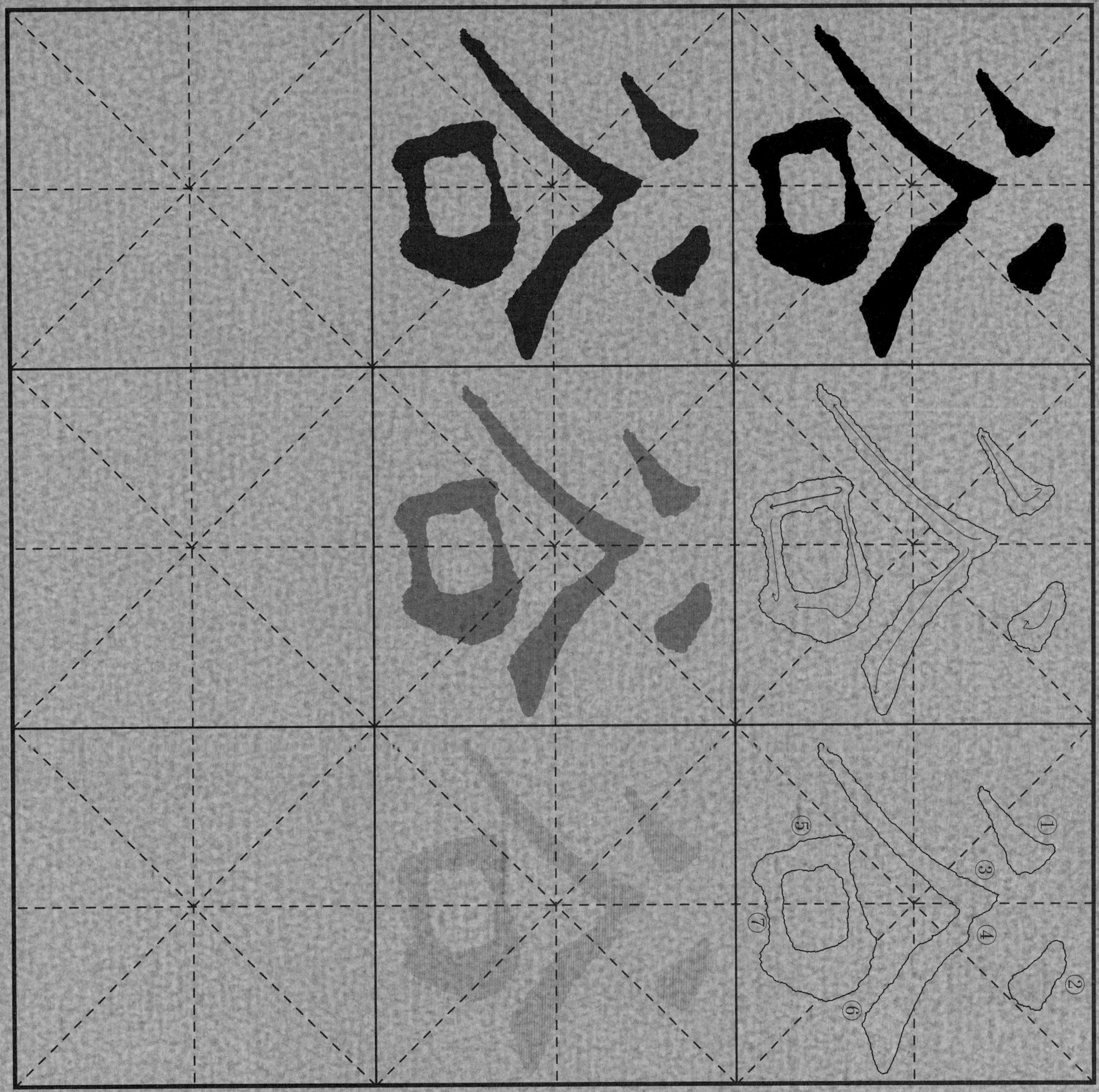
①
②
③
④
⑤
⑥
⑦